The Kingdom Of Light

George Record Peck

THE
KINGDOM OF LIGHT

BY
GEORGE RECORD PECK

G. P. PUTNAM'S SONS
NEW YORK AND LONDON
The Knickerbocker Press
1907

Originally published in *Putnam's Monthly* for
December, 1906

NOTE

THIRTEEN years ago, a few gentle-
men living in or near Milwaukee visited
Phantom Lake, in Waukesha County,
Wisconsin, where beautiful lakes abound.
Their day's outing proved so enjoyable
that they have repeated it yearly ever
since. Inevitably, a club was formed;
and, notwithstanding the pressure for
admission, its membership is still limited
to fourteen. Death and removals have
somewhat altered the personnel of the
Phantom Club, but it remains sub-
stantially the same as it was in 1893.
On their annual outing the members are
in the habit of devoting an evening to

Note

exercises more or less literary in character; and by selecting the best ten or twelve of the papers read on these occasions, they have been able to make up, this year, a slender volume, which has been printed for private distribution only. In this collection the place of honour is deservedly given to the following informal address by George R. Peck, General Counsel of the Chicago, Milwaukee, and St. Paul Railway Company, who has recently retired from the presidency of the American Bar Association. So eloquent an appeal for consideration of the things of the mind and the spirit, comes with special force from the lips of a lawyer immersed in arduous professional labors.

THE EDITORS OF PUTNAM'S MONTHLY.
December, 1906.

The Kingdom of Light

IT is a very beautiful custom which calls this club together each year in midsummer—the sea-'son when Nature is most generous with her ministrations. These are the days when, out of her illimit-able store, she brings beauty and harmony to lives which are, perhaps unconsciously, becoming discord-ant and out of tune. Rest is some-

thing more than the mere ceasing from toil; it is the emancipation of soul and body from care. It is not simply loafing, but loafing with an invitation to the soul, as was Walt Whitman's habit. These literary exercises, which we weave into hours of relaxation, serve to remind us that the world is waiting to receive us back, when our play-spell is over. It would, I suppose, be more in accordance with the current of events, and of ideas which are clamoring continually for expression in these modern days, if I should offer some reflec-

3

tions on themes of immediate and pressing importance. Such themes there are; and by force of circumstances some of them have stared me in the face with a persistency not altogether agreeable. It is not because I underestimate them that I have chosen to ask you to rest for a little while in a serener air. The hungry problems of to-day will have their hearing without asking your permission or mine. The age is restless; it is self-assertive; it is pleased with the sound of its own voice, and confident in the strength of its own

arm. And yet, there are doubts
and misgivings in the minds of
thoughtful men, who find themselves dumb to the questions they
cannot help asking. When social
and economic problems press upon
us almost constantly; when the
men of labour and the men of capital count themselves as belonging
to separate classes, and neither
trusts the other; when the mys-
teries of supply and demand, the
prospect of coming crops, the out-
look for trade, and the hazards of
business are with men by night
and by day, we may be sure that

7

the highly artificial mechanism we call civilisation is liable almost any day to some painful dislocation.

But of these things it is not my purpose to speak. I allude to them, because, as it seems to me, every one must be sensible of their importance, and must feel that their shadow is never lifted, save for little intervals—and, may I not add, upon an occasion such as this?

Fellow Phantoms, it is probably not your habit to call yourselves philosophers, but nevertheless I

suspect that each of you nurses a
consoling belief that he is one. It
is this opinion which gives to men
of your age that little air of con-
descension, that tone of gentle
patronage, as if to say, "See how
much I know about life and its
duties." But while you are listening to these sweet self-commenda-
tions, you might perhaps hear
some unanointed outsider remark:
"Yes, doubtless you are a philosopher ; but if you are so very
wise, why have you so little to
show for it?" Ah! that is the
question. How many centuries is

The Kingdom of Light

it since Plato was writing those immortal dialogues which have bewitched the minds of men from his age to ours, but leave us still struggling to make knowledge and conduct go hand in hand, and wisdom and character true reflections of each other? Nothing is so easy as to state sound ethical doctrines,—nothing so difficult as to live up to them. I suppose that more than half the literature in the world consists of good advice, —the rest is the story of many stumblings by the way, many mistakes, many failures, with here

and there glimpses which leave
but little save the ever unsatisfied
inquiry—

Whither has fled the visionary gleam?
Where is it now, the glory and the
    dream?

Ah! if there were some method of
living by which we could keep the
glory and the dream, the problem
would be solved. When I think of
the mistakes you have probably
made, and of those I have certainly
made, I surrender the position of
philosopher and can only stammer,
with George Eliot's Theophrastus

Such, "Dear blunderers, I am one
of you."

Some of us will perhaps never
be wiser than we are now. I wish
I could be sure we shall never
be less wise. Wisdom has a habit
of her own; she lingers while the
years speed onward toward our
common destination.

It is not for me to enter the
domain of religion, nor to trench
upon ground occupied by men who
have been specially called to the
work. I speak only of the life that
now is; how its highest compensa-
tions can be won, its rewards, if

you please, attained; its sorrows
mitigated, and its joys increased
and multiplied.

And this is the lesson I would
give: Dwell in the Kingdom of
Light. And where is that kingdom? What are its boundaries?
What cities are builded within it?
What hills, and plains, and mountain slopes gladden the eyes of its
possessors? Be patient, my fellow
Phantoms. Do not hasten to
search for it. It is here. The
Kingdom of Light, like the Kingdom of God, is within you. And
what do I mean by the Kingdom

The Kingdom of Light

of Light? I mean that realm of which a quaint old poet sang those quaint old lines:

> My mind to me a kingdom is,—
> Such perfect joy therein I find,
> As far exceeds all earthly bliss.

I mean that invisible commonwealth which outlives the storms of ages ; that state whose armaments are thoughts ; whose weapons are ideas ; whose trophies are the pages of the world's great masters.

The Kingdom of Light is the kingdom of the intellect, of the

imagination, of the heart, of the spirit and the things of the spirit. And why, perhaps you are asking, do you make this appeal to us? How dare you intimate that we are not already dedicated to high purposes, and enrolled among those who stand for the nobler and better things of human life? Take it not unkindly if I tell you frankly that a little plainness of speech will not hurt even such as we. All experience has shown that it is at our age, or thereabouts, that men are most prone to grow weary. It is not in the morning of the march,

23

but in the afternoon, that soldiers
find it most difficult to keep step
with the column that follows the
colours.

I have appealed to you for what
I have called the intellectual life.
By the intellectual life I mean
that course of living which recog-
nises always and without ceasing
the infinite value of the mind;
which gives to its cultivation and
to its enlargement a constant
and enduring devotion; and which
clings to it in good and in evil
days with a growing and abiding
love.

The Kingdom of Light

The Kingdom of Light is open to all who *seek* the light. This may appear a mere truism, since every one admits the superiority of the mental over the physical nature. But that is where the danger lies. All admit it; but how few act upon it! How many men and women do you know who after they have, as the phrase goes, finished their education, ever give a serious thought to their mental growth? They have no time; no time to live, but only to exist. Do not misunderstand me. I do not expect, nor do I think it possible,

that the great majority of people can make intellectual improvement their first or only aim. God's wisdom has made the law that man must dig and delve, must work with his hands and bend his back to the burden that is laid upon it. We must have bread; but how inexpressibly foolish it is to suppose we can live by bread alone.

Granting all that can be claimed for lack of time, for the food and clothing to be bought, and the debts to be paid, the truth remains —and I beg you to remember it,—

the person who allows his mental
and spiritual nature to stagnate
and decay does so not for want of
time, but for want of inclination.
The farm, the shop, and the office
are not such hard masters as we
imagine. We yield too easily to
their sway, and set them up as
rulers when they ought to be only
servants. There is no vocation — absolutely none — that
cuts off entirely the opportu-
nities for intellectual develop-
ment. The Kingdom of Light
is an especially delightful home
for him whose purse is not of

sufficient weight to provide a home elsewhere, and a humble cottage in the Kingdom can be made to shine with a brightness above palace walls. For my part I would rather have been Charles Lamb than the Duke of Wellington, and his influence in the world is incalculably the greater of the two. And yet he was but a clerk in the India House, poor in pocket, but rich beyond measure in his very poverty, whose jewels are not in the goldsmith's list. The problem of life is to rightly adjust the prose to the

poetry, the sordid to the spiritual,
the common and selfish to the high
and beneficent, forgetting not that
these last are incomparably the
more precious.

Modern life is a startling con-
tradiction. Never were colleges so
numerous, so prosperous, so richly
endowed as now. Never were
public schools so well conducted,
or so largely patronised. But yet,
what Carlyle perhaps too bitterly
calls "the mechanical spirit of
the age" is upon us. The com-
mercial spirit, too, is with us,
holding its head so high that

timid souls are frightened at its pretensions. It is the scholar's duty to set his face resolutely against both.

I can never be the apostle of despair. The colours in the morning and the evening sky are brilliant yet. But I fear the scholar is not the force he once was, and will again be when the twentieth century gets through its carnival of invention and construction. We have culture; what we need is the love of culture. We have knowledge; but our prayer should be, "Give us the love of knowledge."

37

The Kingdom of Light

I may be wrong, but I sometimes wish Nature would be more stingy of her secrets. She has given them out with so lavish a hand that some men think the greatest thing in the world is to persuade her to work in some newly invented harness. Edison and the other wizards of science have almost succeeded in making life automatic. Its chord is set to a minor key. Plain living and high thinking, that once went together, are transformed into high living and very plain thinking. The old-time simplicity of manners, the modest

tastes of our fathers, have given
way to the clang and clash, the
noise and turbulence, that char-
acterise the age. We know too
much—and too little. We know
the law of evolution; but who can
tell us when, or how, or why it
came to be the law? We accept it as
a great scientific truth, and as such
it should be welcomed. But life has
lost something of its zest, some of
the glory that used to be in it, since
we were told that mind is only an
emanation of matter, a force or
principle mechanically produced by
molecular motion within the brain.

The Kingdom of Light

When the telephone burst upon us a few years ago, the world was delighted and amazed. And yet we were not needing telephones half as much as we were needing men; men who, by living above the common level, should exalt and dignify human life. I sometimes think it would be wise to close the Patent Office in Washington, and to say to the tired brains of the inventors, "Rest, and be refreshed." We hurry on to new devices which shall be ears to the deaf, and eyes to the blind, and feet to the halt; but meantime the

43

poems are unwritten, and hearts
that are longing for one strain of
the music they used to hear are
told to be satisfied with the
great achievements of the past
century. The wisest of the Greeks
taught that the ideal is the
only true real ; and Emerson, our
American seer, who sent forth
from Concord his inspiring oracles,
taught the same. I may be wrong,
but I cannot help thinking that
neither here nor hereafter does
salvation lie in wheat, or corn, or
iron.

Again I must plead that you

take my words as I mean them. I do not preach a gospel of mere sentiment, nor of inane, impracticable dilettanteism. The Lord put it in my way to learn long ago that we cannot eat poetry, or art, or sunbeams. And yet I hold it true, now and always, that life without these things is shorn of more than half its value. The ox and his master differ little in dignity if neither rises above the level of the stomach or the manger.

The highest use of the mind is not mere logic, the almost mechanical function of drawing conclu-

47

sions from facts. Even lawyers do
that; and so, also, to some extent,
as naturalists tell us, do the horse
and the dog. The human intellect
is best used when its possessor
suffers it to reach out beyond its
own environment into the realm
where God has placed truth and
beauty and the influences that
make for righteousness. There is
no such thing as a common or
humdrum life, unless we make it
so ourselves. The rainbow and the
rose will give their colours to all
alike. The sense of beauty that is
born in every soul pleads for per-

49

mission to remain there. Cast it out, and not all the cunning of an Edison can replace it.

It is the imagination, or perhaps I should say the imaginative faculty, that most largely separates man from the lower animals, and that also divides the higher from the lower order of men. We all respect the multiplication table, and find in it about the only platform upon which we can agree to stand; but he would be a curiously incomplete man to whose soul it would bring the rapture that comes from reading *Hamlet* or

The Kingdom of Light

In Memoriam. The thoughts that console and elevate are not those the world calls practical. Even in the higher walks of science, where the mind enlarges to the scope of Newton's and Kepler's great discoveries, the demonstrated truth is not the whole truth, nor the best truth. As Professor Everett, of Harvard, has finely said in a recent work: "Science only gives us hints of what, by a higher method, we come to know. The astronomer tells us he has swept the heavens with his telescope and found no God." But "the eye of the soul"

outsweeps the telescope, and finds, not only in the heavens, but everywhere, the presence that is eternal. The reverent soul, seeking for the power that makes for righteousness, will not find it set down in scientific formula. I hold it to be the true office of culture—if I may use that much-derided word—to stimulate the higher intellectual faculties; to give the mind something of that perfection which is found in finely tuned instruments that need only to be touched to give back noble and responsive melody. There is a music that has

55

never been named; and yet so deep a meaning has it, that the very stars keep time to its celestial rhythm.

There 's not the smallest orb which thou
    behold'st,
But in his motion like an angel sings,
Still quiring to the young-eyed cher-
    ubins;
Such harmony is in immortal souls.

The dwellers in the Kingdom of Light have a steadfast love for things that cannot be computed, nor reckoned, nor measured. In the daily papers you may read the latest quotations of stocks and bonds, but once upon a time a

little band of listeners heard the words, "Are not two sparrows sold for a farthing?" and went away with a lesson that Wall Street has yet to learn.

And now you are scornfully asking: "Do you expect men to earn money by following these shadowy and intangible sentiments, which, however noble, are not yet current at the store and market? We must eat, though poetry and art and music perish from the earth." Yes, so it would seem, but *only* seem. I cannot tell *why*, but I am sure that he who

59

remembers that something divine
is mixed in him with the clay, will
find the way open for both the
divine and the earthly. You will
not starve for following the Light.
But I beg of you to remember that
this is not a question of incomes
and profits. The things I plead
for are not set down in ledgers.
How hard to think of the un-
selfish and the ultimate, instead
of the personal and immediate.
Even unto Jesus they came and
inquired, "Who is the greatest in
the Kingdom of Heaven?" It is not
strange, then, that we do not give

up personal advantage here. But in the Kingdom of Light, in the life I am saying we ought to lead, nothing can be taken from us that can be compared with what we shall receive.

It is quite likely we may be poor, though I am afraid we shall not be, for in the twentieth century no man is safe from sudden wealth; but a worse calamity might befall us than poverty. St. Francis of Assisi, as Renan has said, was, next to Jesus, the sweetest soul that ever walked this earth, and he condemned himself to hunger and

rags. I do not advise you to follow him through the lonely forest, and into the shaded glen where the birds used to welcome him to be their friend and companion; but I do most assuredly think it better to live as he did, on bread and water and the cresses that grow by the mountain spring, than to give up the glory and joys of the higher life. In the Kingdom of Light there are friendships of inestimable value; friendships that are rest unto the body, and solace to the soul that is troubled. When Socrates was condemned, how promptly

The Kingdom of Light

his spirit rose to meet the de-
cree of the judges, as he told them
of the felicity he should find in
the change that would give him
the opportunity of listening to the
enchanting converse of Orpheus
and Musæus and Hesiod and
Homer.

Such companionship is ours,
through the instrumentality of
books. Here, even in this Western
land, the worthies of every age will
come to our firesides; will travel
with us on the distant journey; will
abide with us wherever our lot
may be cast. And the smaller the

orbit in which we move, the more contracted the scale of our personal relations, the more valuable and the more needful are those sweet relationships which James Martineau so aptly calls " the friendships of history." In a strain of unrivalled elevation of thought and purity of language, he says:

He that cannot leave his workshop or his village, let him have his passport to other centuries, and find communion in a distant age; it will enable him to look up into those silent faces that cannot deceive, and take the hand of solemn guidance that will never mislead or betray. The ground-plot of a man's own destiny may be closely shut in, and

the cottage of his rest small; but if the
story of this Old World be not quite
strange to him—if he can find his way
through its vanished cities to hear the
pleadings of justice or watch the worship
of the gods; if he can visit the battle-fields
where the infant life of nations has been
baptised in blood; if he can steal into
the prisons where the lonely martyrs
have waited for their death; if he can
walk in the garden or beneath the porch
where the lovers of wisdom discourse,
or be a guest at the banquet where the
wine of high converse pa ses around; if
the experience of his own country and
the struggles that consecrate the very
soil beneath his feet are no secret to
him; if he can listen to Latimer at Paul's
Cross, and tend the wounded Hampden
in the woods at Chalgrove, and gaze,
as upon familiar faces, at the portraits

71

The Kingdom of Light

of More and Bacon, of Vane and Cromwell, of Owen, Fox, and Baxter—he consciously belongs to a grander life than could be given by territorial possession; he venerates an ancestry auguster than a race of kings; and is richer in the sources of character than any prince or monarch.

Some there are, no doubt, who believe that intellectual culture does not make men better or happier, and that the conscience and moral faculties are set apart from merely mental attributes. But surely you have not accepted such a false and narrow view. Unless colleges are a foolish and expensive

73

luxury; unless civilisation is worth-
less; unless the centuries that have
witnessed the upward stride of
humanity have been wasted; unless the savage, chattering incanta-
tions to his fetich, is a nobler
product of the race than a Milton,
a Wilberforce, an Emerson, or a
Lowell, then heart and mind,
morality and education, *do* go
together in true and loyal companionship. The trouble of to-day,
as I have tried to show, is not that
we have too much culture, but
too much bending of the knee to
purely material results; too much

worship of the big and not enough | ✓
of the great.

It is the fate of most of us to
work either with hand or brain;
but even in this short life a success-
fully conducted bank, or a bridge
that you have built, or a lawsuit
you have won, have in themselves
little of special significance or value.
Very common men have done all
these things. When I hear the
glorification of the last twenty
years, of the fields subdued, the
roads rebuilt, the fortunes accu-
mulated, the factories started, I
say to myself: "All these are good,

but not so good that we should
make ourselves hoarse with huzzas,
or that we should suppose for a
moment they belong to the higher
order of achievements." Sometimes, too, when I hear the noisy
clamour over some great difficulty
that has been conquered, I think
of James Wolfe under the walls of
Quebec, repeating sadly those lines
of Gray's *Elegy:*

The boast of heraldry, the pomp of
    pow'r,
  And all that beauty, all that wealth
    e'er gave,
Await alike th' inevitable hour:
  The paths of glory lead but to the
    grave.

79

The Kingdom of Light

And I think also how he turned to his officers with that pathetic prevision of the death that was to come to-morrow on the Heights of Abraham and said, "I would rather have written that poem than to take Quebec." And he was right.

Indeed, if we but knew it, the citadel that crowns the mountain's brow—nay, the mountains themselves, ancient, rugged, motionless, —are but toys compared with the silent, invisible, but eternal structure of God's greatest handiwork, the mind.

The Kingdom of Light

I pray you remember there is,
if we but search for it, something
ennobling in every vocation; in
every enterprise which engages the
efforts of man. Do you think
Michael Angelo reared the dome,
and painted those immortal fres-
coes, simply because he had a con-
tract to do so? Was the soldier
who died at Marathon or Gettys-
burg thinking of the wages the
state had promised him? Be assured that, whatever fate may
befall us, nothing so bad can come
as to sink into that wretched existence where everything is for-

The Kingdom of Light

gotten but the profit of the hour:
the food, the raiment, the handful
of silver, the ribbon to wear on the
coat. It is but an old story I am
telling; but I console myself with
the reflection that it cannot be
told too often, and only by telling
is it kept fresh in the memory and
in the heart. The world will go on
buying and selling, hoping and
fearing, loving and hating, and we
shall be in the throng; but in God's
name let us not turn away from
the Light, nor from the Kingdom
that is in the midst of the Light.

In every street shadows are

85

walking who were once brave, hopeful and confident. Nay! they are not shadows, but ghosts, dead years ago, in everything but the mere physical portion of existence. They go through the regular operations of trade and traffic, the office, and the court; but they are not living men. They are but bones and skeletons rattling along in a melancholy routine, which has in it neither life nor the spirit of life. It is a sad picture, but saddest because it is true. They knew what happy days were, when they walked in pleasant paths and

felt in their hearts the freshness of
spring. But contact with the world
was too much for them. Hesita-
tion and doubt drove out loyalty
and faith. They listened to the
voice of worldly wisdom as Othello
listened to Iago, and the end of
the story is,

> Put out the light, and then—put out the
> light.

The dwellers in the Kingdom of
which I am speaking are hostages
to art and letters, to high aims and
noble destinies. They may forget,
they may be false, but if some are
not faithful, truth and liberty and

the best of civilisation will be lost,
or in danger of being lost. In every
ship that sails there must be some
to stay by the craft; some to speak
the word of cheer; some to soothe
the fears of the timorous and
affrighted. When Paul was jour-
neying to Italy on that memorable
voyage which changed the destinies of the world, the mariners
were frightened as the storm
came on, and were casting the
boats over to seek safety, they
knew not whither; but Paul said
to the centurion and to the
soldiers, "Except these abide in

the ship, ye cannot be saved."

It is because I believe so strongly in the saving power of the intellectual life upon the institutions of society, and upon the welfare of individuals, that I plead so earnestly for it. The fortunes of science, art, literature, and government are indissolubly ·linked with it. The centres and shrines of the most potent influences are not the seats of commerce and capital. The village of Concord, where Emerson, Hawthorne, Alcott, and Thoreau lived, was, in their day, and will long continue

93

to be a greater force in this nation than New York and Chicago added to each other. Let us rest in the assured faith that, whoever may *seem* to rule, the thinker is, and always will be, the master.

Those of you who have read Auerbach's great novel remember the motto from Goethe on the title-page,—

On every height there lies repose.

Rest!—how eagerly we seek it! How sweet it is when we are tired of the fret and worry of life! But remember, I pray you, that it

The Kingdom of Light

dwells above the level, in the serene element that reaches to the infinities. Only there is heard the music of the choir invisible; only there can we truly know the rest, the peace, and the joy of those who dwell in the Kingdom of Light.

THE END

97

CPSIA information can be obtained
at www.ICGtesting.com
Printed in the USA
BVHW071040060820
585686BV00010B/785